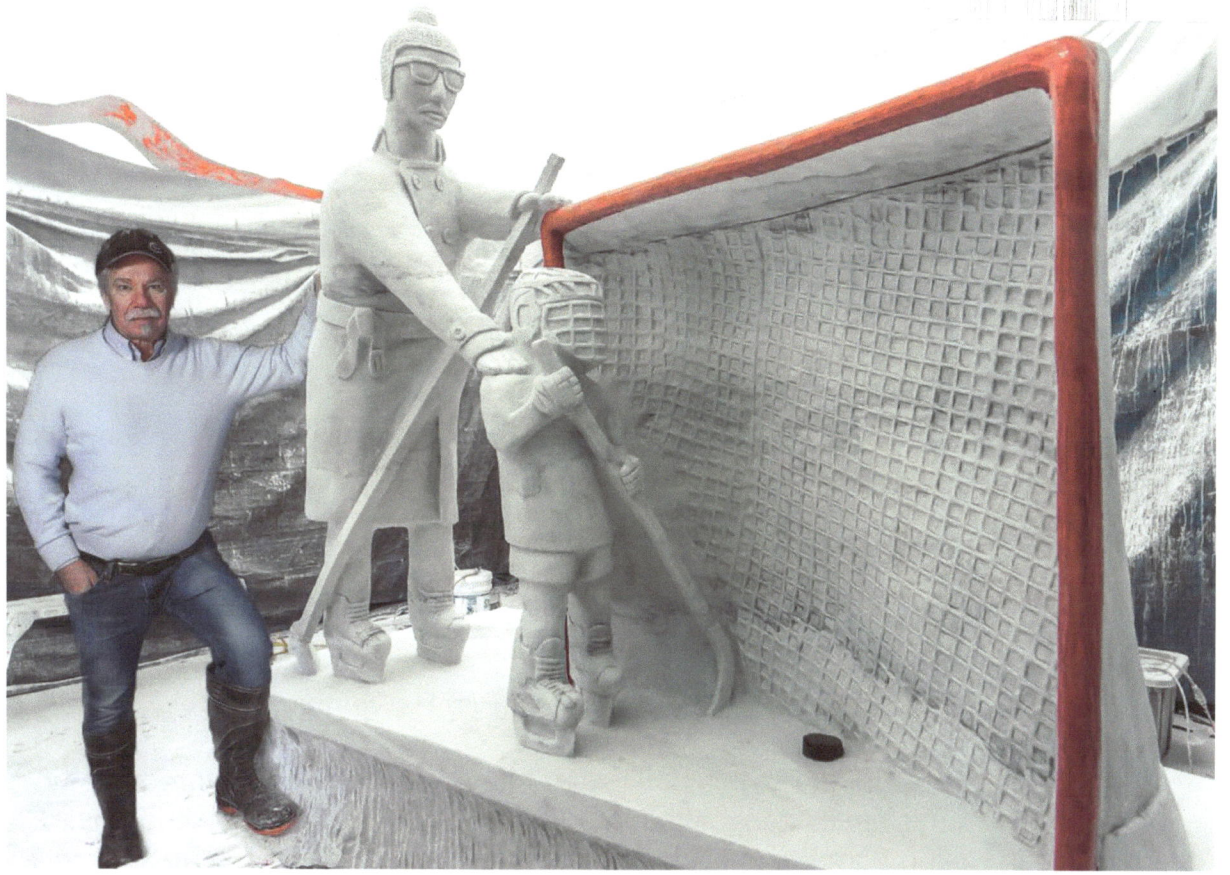

The "Creating a Champion" Story

An adventure - From Start to Finish!!

J.W. (Bill) Harvey
www.willieangelo.com

Copyright © 2022 by J.W. (Bill) Harvey

All rights reserved. No part of this publication may be reproduced, stored in any form of retrieval system or transmitted in any form or by any means without prior permission in writing from the publishers except for the use of brief quotations in a book review.

ISBN:
Paperback: 9798798714872

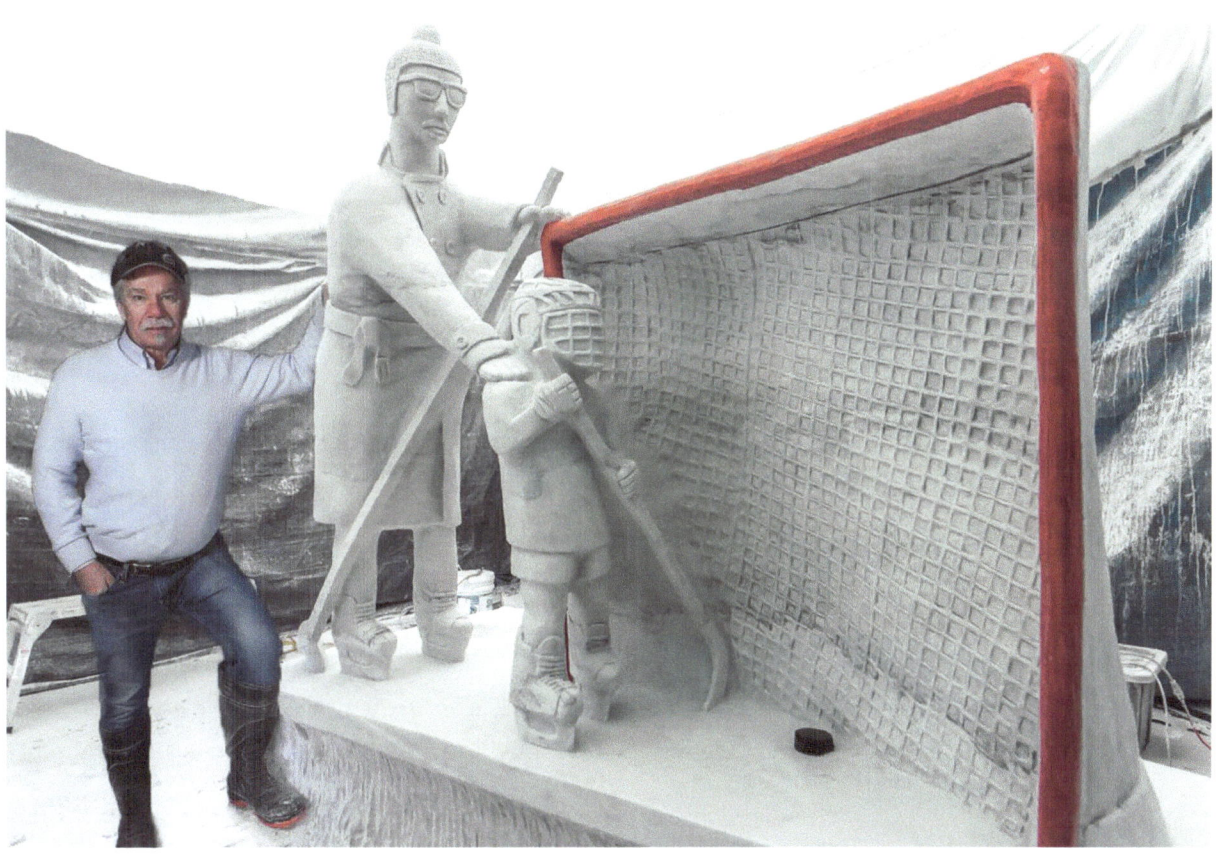

This is a story that, like so many, started as a silly thought! A thought of Michelangelo …… that thought developed over time …… ultimately turning into this 4 ton sculpture. This "Creating a Champion" design came to me in an instant ….. an instant of panic that I will also describe later. Champion is carved into a single 12 ton block of Canadian white marble from a quarry on Vancouver Island, BC, Canada.

In the hundreds of hours grinding away on this rock, another thought came to me ….. I wonder how Walter Gretzky thinks back on those first days on the ice with Wayne Gretzky in Brantford Ontario Canada ….. Walter coaching his newbie hockey son ….. what pride he must experience today!! …… in any case, whether I saw an actual photo of them or whether it was my imaginings ……

Voila! ….. "Creating a Champion"

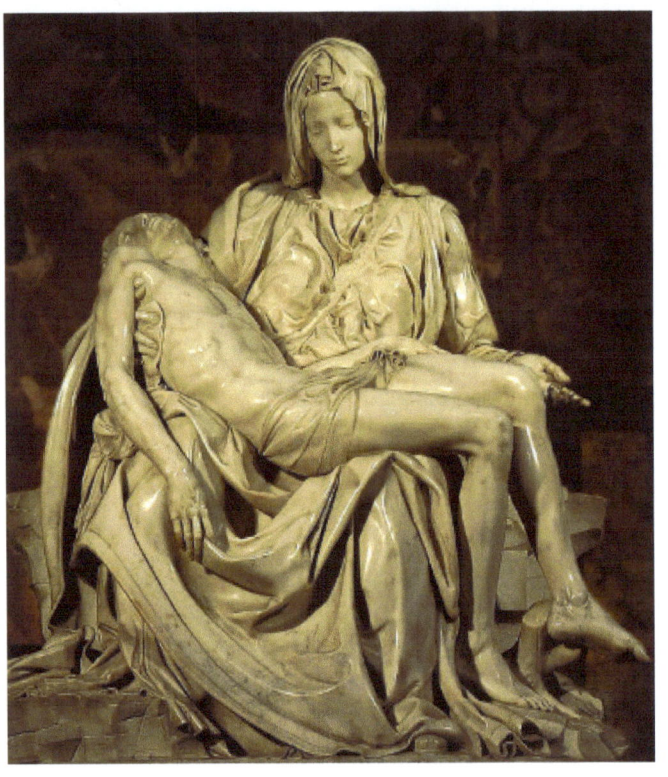

The genesis of Creating a Champion – the idea of creating a life size marble sculpture has its origin back in 1974. My girlfriend Mona (later wife and later yet ex-wife) and I traveled through Europe …… we visited the Vatican in Rome, Italy and were fortunate enough to see Michelangelo's Pieta. My recollection from that time was that the Pieta was a particularly beautiful sculpture …… I was 22 years old in 1974 and it was clearly an emotional experience that has stayed with me ….. it is impossible to understand this kind of beauty without actually seeing the sculpture ……… 33 years later the thought came to mind of doing something myself ….. more on this later!

Why Willieangelo.com? When I first started this project everyone thought I was absolutely crazy …... especially when they saw the size of my 44,000 pound rock. My friend Ken started calling me Willieangelo when I told him the story of seeing Michelangelo's Pieta ….. my thought …… "willieangelo" ….. sounds like a good "brand" ….. why not just go with that as the name of my website ….. www.willieangelo.com. On that site I describe the "Creating a Champion" story and the sculpture projects that I have undertaken over the years ….

I have lived a lot ….. From Alberta …… to British Columbia ….. to California ….. and back ….. this is another one of those stories!!!

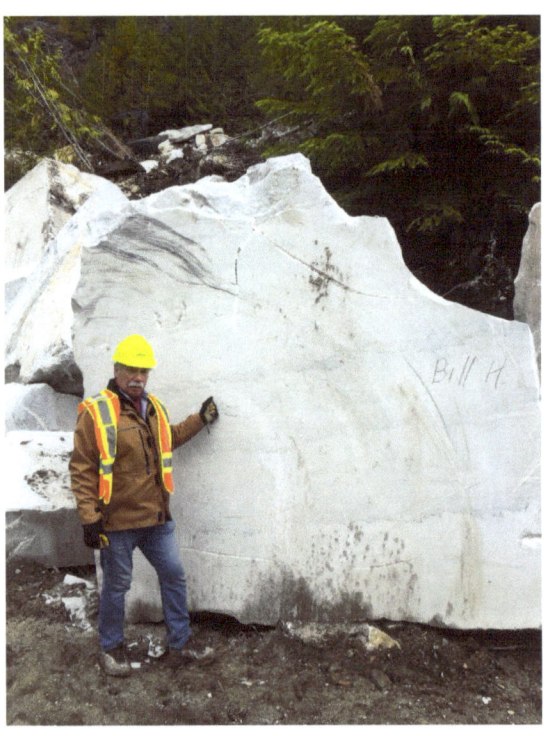

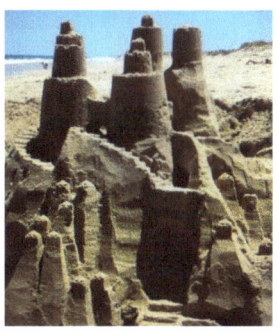

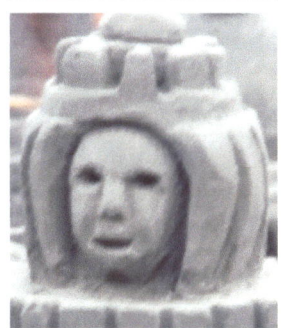

How did you learn sculpture? Many have asked me that ….. My answer ….. The Nike school of ….. "Just Do It" ….. I have been described as being "eclectic" and I think that might fit how I have "just done" a lot of things …... some with success and some failures ……. Building sand castles was the start of my sculpting. Later my first attempt at a real sculptural element in the White Rock BC sand castle contest. It was the Queen of Hearts from the "Alice Through the Looking Glass" story …. Built out of sand, she was one piece on a 40 ft x 40 ft sand chess board. With the next high tide, the whole thing was reclaimed by the Salish Sea …… many years later the thought of doing a marble sculpture occurred to me.

Real Sculpture – In 2007 I was staying at my brother's BnB near Revelstoke BC alongside the Eagle River. Bald eagles fly there quite often and I thought that it would be nice to have the sculpture of an eagle on the property. So I just started and created my first one out of red cedar (my Sister-in-Law later painted it pink – I love it) ……. Later that year I did the Sitting Eagle at my sister's place on the Sunshine Coast and then in the Spring of 2010 I decided to do a life size "Eagle Flying" ….. the piece was given to a friend to mount in her cabin in Northern Alberta.

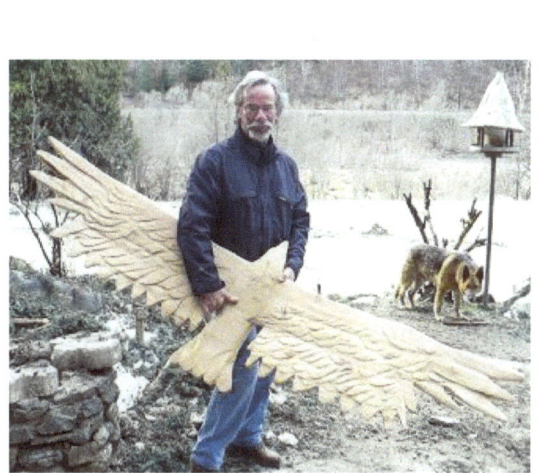

It was while I was carving "Eagle Flying" that the thought came to me of the work Michelangelo did on his various sculptures, including the Pieta …. how extraordinary it is ….. how they worked with hammers and chisels to actually create the form of the sculpture ……. they then used pumice and emery stones to polish the sculpture to a level of beauty that is awe inspiring

I was certainly awed back in 1974 ….. I asked myself ….. "if Michelangelo and his team could produce those pieces with hammers and chisels, what could I do today with modern power tools"? ….. that question was the seed that became "Creating a Champion"

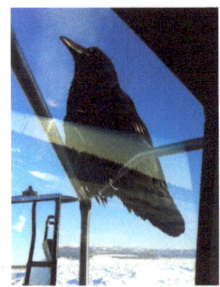 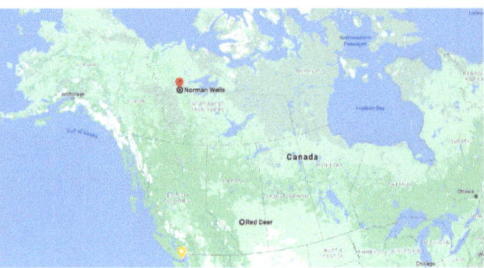 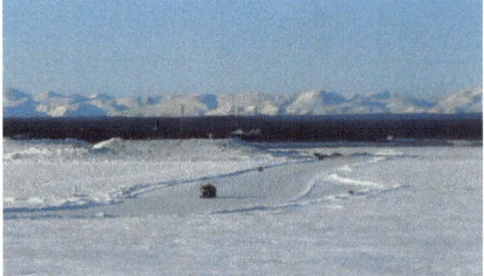

In 2012 the thought of carving something in marble returned while I was working at Norman Wells, NWT. Norman Wells is a little hamlet along the Mackenzie River, about 60 kilometers from the Arctic Circle. Part of that work was building the ice roads across the Mackenzie River (yes just like the TV show - LOL) to access man-made islands where Esso extracted their oil and shipped it south by pipeline.

We had lots of free time and the thought of carving in marble resurfaced. I was living in Victoria BC at this time and I learned that there were marble quarries on Vancouver Island. The thought ….. "Humm ….. why not give it a go and try carving some marble".

Angel is approximately 8 inches tall.

Matrix Marble in Duncan BC had some sample rocks that they gave me to experiment with. I did my first piece in pink marble ….. called Angel ….. the design started with an idea of having a battle between the Archangel and the devil …… it became clear very quickly that the 20 lb rock would not allow for my envisioned design ……. (more about sculpture design and the rock "allowing" later). My daughter has Angel ……

Lady of the Lake is about 20 inches tall.

In 2014 I got a 60 lb piece of grey marble and carved what I called "Lady of the Lake" …… I gave her to another friend in Calgary.

Fast forward another few years to 2018 and a new job working for another oilfield services company, Calfrac Well Services in Red Deer Alberta. Oil prices are falling and Calfrac decides to cut our work schedule from working 2 weeks on and 1 week off to 2 weeks on and 2 weeks off …… sheeshhh!!!! ….. my thoughts "what the heck am I going to do with two weeks off every month?" ….. well as you might imagine, the old idea re-surfaced and along with "you have time, you have money" …… why not ….. "Just Do It"

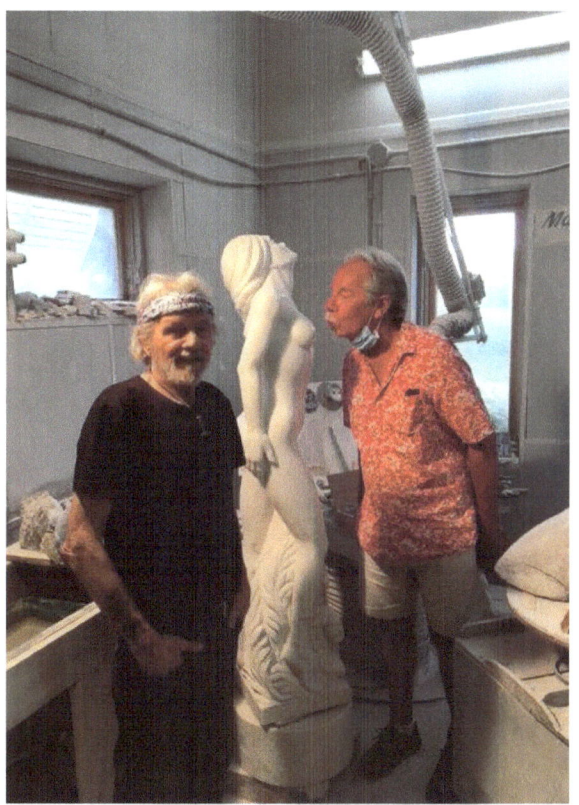

So what started as "I can do this" ….. maybe as an art project ….. maybe an ego thing …….. or maybe it is a "blood memory" thing …. the idea being that we have memories in our blood that stem from our long lost pasts ….. thoughts that drive us to "just do it"

It turns out that sculpture is in Harvey blood from centuries past …… it has been part of my long lost heritage …… my ancestors have been sculptors of wood and marble dating back to the 1700s in Quebec and earlier in France……

I only learned of this heritage during my recent 6 month stay in Quebec City. I met Maurice Harvey in June of 2021, (on the left https://mauharvey.com/) He and I share relatives who lived in Quebec in the 1600 and 1700s …… many of them accomplished sculptors. We learned of our genealogical connections through my direct cousin Albert Lebeau …. a Quebecois relation on my father's side.

In any case …… back to Champion ….. first step …. find some marble ….. I knew of the Matrix Marble quarry on Vancouver Island so my first call was to them ….. their quote ….. $1.00 per pound ….. huuummmm??? ….. Angel would have cost $15 or so ….. Lady would have cost $60 or so …… if I want to do something lifesize …… uhhhhhhh …. $40,000 …… impossible …… I am not wealthy and there is no way I could do that ….. I needed to find a block that would be big enough to do something lifesize ….. what was I to do?

So more research …… I found another quarry called Pacific West Stone ….. I called their manager …… asked if I could come visit the mine and look over their "seconds"….. they agreed …… and so the "Creating a Champion" adventure began ….. then on my next days off …… (remember I have two weeks) …… I jump in my little red Toyota Yaris …… 1,546 km from Red Deer Alberta to the quarry on the north end of Vancouver Island.

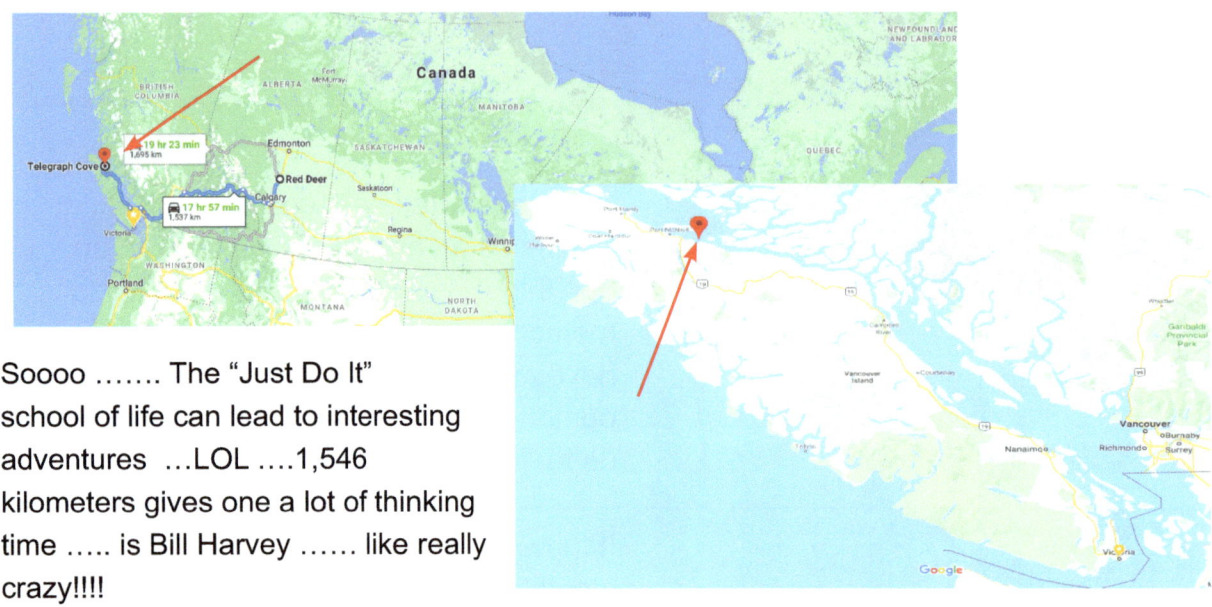

Soooo ……. The "Just Do It" school of life can lead to interesting adventures …LOL ….1,546 kilometers gives one a lot of thinking time ….. is Bill Harvey …… like really crazy!!!!

The Pacific West Stone quarry is located on Vancouver Island in the Bonanza Mountain Range southeast of Telegraph Cove, which is in turn southeast of Port Hardy on Vancouver Island, British Columbia, Canada …… awesome scenery!

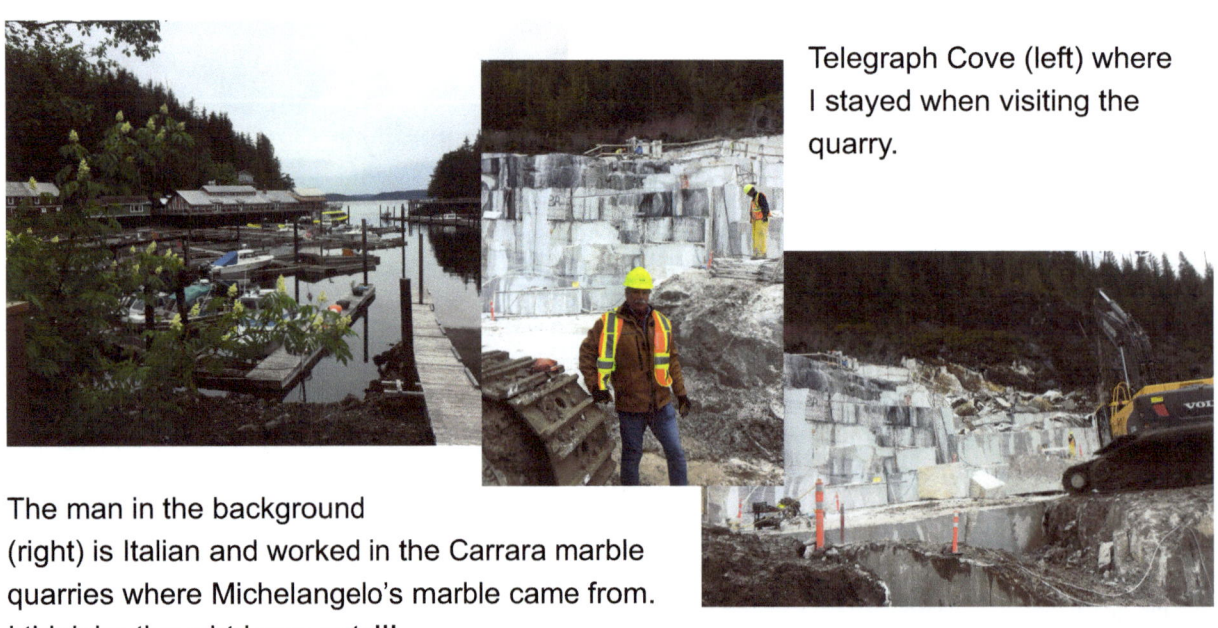

Telegraph Cove (left) where I stayed when visiting the quarry.

The man in the background (right) is Italian and worked in the Carrara marble quarries where Michelangelo's marble came from. I think he thought I was nuts!!!

Pacific Stone cuts marble blocks and sells them to manufacturers who, in turn, cut them into marble counter tops and marble tiles etc …… the rock needs to be perfect for those products so anything that isn't good enough for their market is just pushed off to the edge of the quarry. The quarry manager and I scrambled over hundreds of these marble boulders looking …… looking for the right rock and …… VOILA!!!! I don't know why but this particular block "jumped out" and said "Take me, take me!!!" So the manager wrote my name on it and the reality began to come into focus ….. LOL!!

I now own a 44,000 lb rock!!!

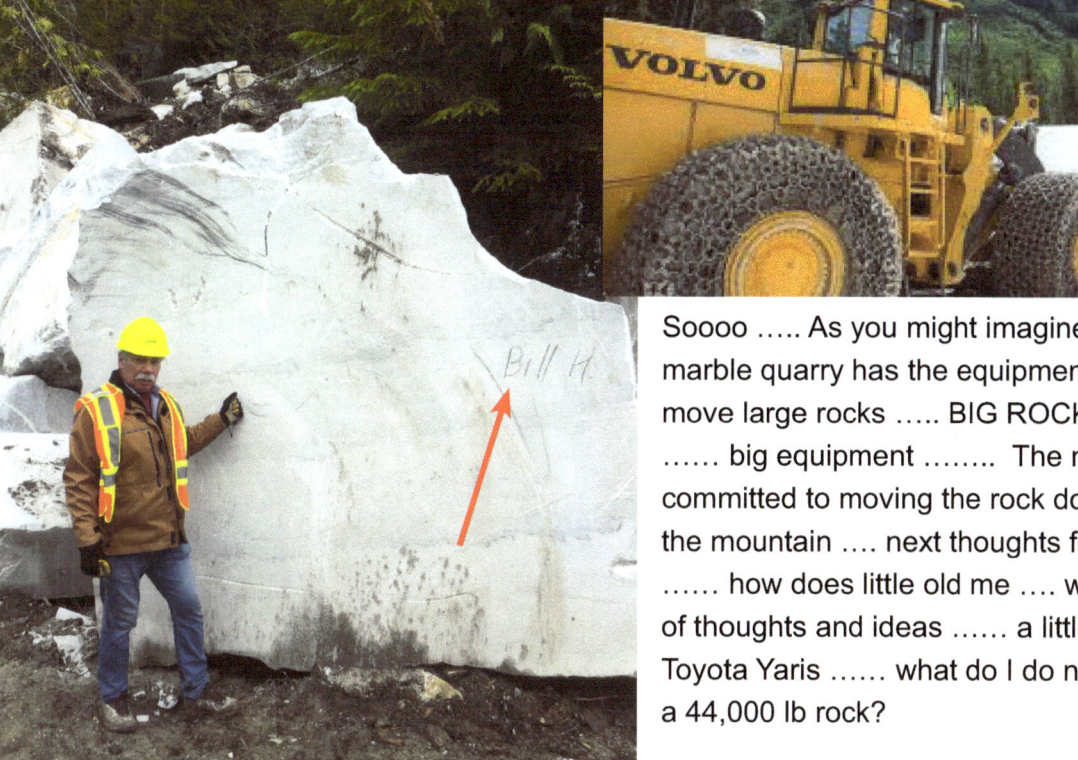

Soooo ….. As you might imagine a marble quarry has the equipment to move large rocks ….. BIG ROCKS …… big equipment …….. The mine committed to moving the rock down the mountain …. next thoughts for me …… how does little old me …. with a lot of thoughts and ideas …… a little red Toyota Yaris …… what do I do now with a 44,000 lb rock?

I drove back to Red Deer …… another 1,540 kms …… and lots more thinking time
 …… lots more thoughts!

I did not know what I did not know!! ….. what obstacles am I really facing? ….. should I do some of the carving at the quarry to reduce the weight before transporting? …. do I hire a trucking company to move it? …. do I rent a pickup truck and trailer? …. where do I actually do the carving when it gets to Red Deer? ….. how do I get it off the trailer in Red Deer? …. what tools will I need to actually do this carving? …. imagine all of this stuff and more banging around in my head ….. while driving back the 1,546 km ….. at work over the next two weeks ….. I finally decide that I would figure out how to truck it home to Red Deer …..

My Imagination crashes into My Reality

So I started wondering what would I do with that stone. What kind of sculpture ….. what would the subject matter be? ….. who might want to have such a piece when it was completed? …..

I started to think of the hockey industry. There was a brand new arena being built in Calgary …… there were several in the NHL being planned ….. there might be some NHL owner or even some of the players that might want it …… I settled on a hockey theme! …… came up with a preliminary design that I thought might be doable! ….. Little did I know ….

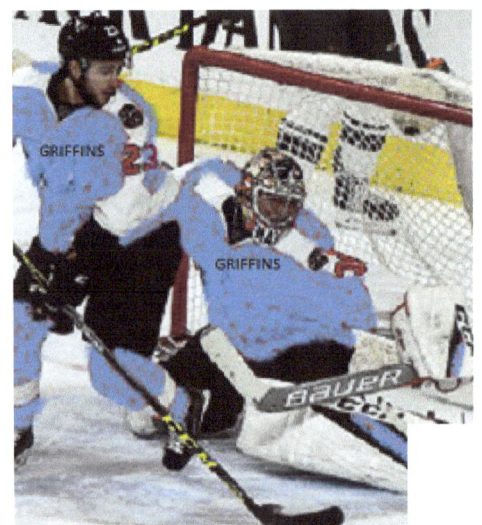

I had inspected my 44,000 pound rock for all of 15 to 20 minutes prior to making a commitment. As I mentioned earlier, I had lots of time to concoct a vision of what I might be able to carve into that monster rock. Left is the image I used as a basis for an illustrator to come up with an initial design sketch (below).

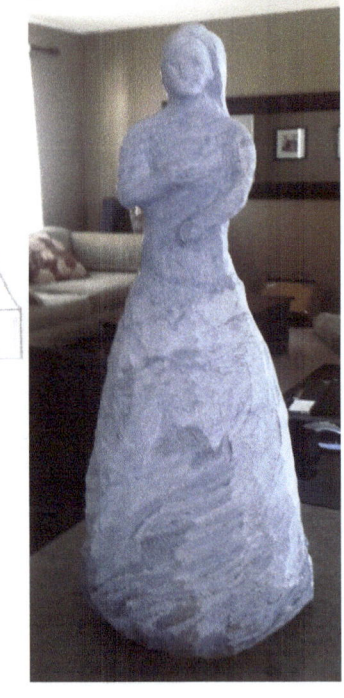

Now remember that prior to choosing "My Rock" ….. the biggest and most complex thing that I had ever done was the very simple Lady of the Lake. She is about 22-26 inches tall and weighs about 25 lbs. I had no idea what it meant to work with a 44,000 lb rock ….. A rock that is 12 feet wide by 10 feet tall and 5 feet deep …. what have I got myself into??

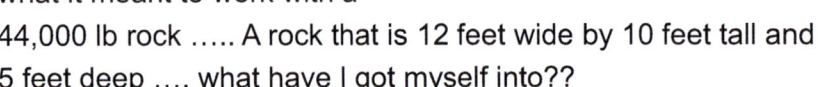
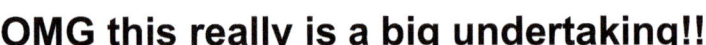

OMG this really is a big undertaking!!

Imaginings, Reality, Artistry

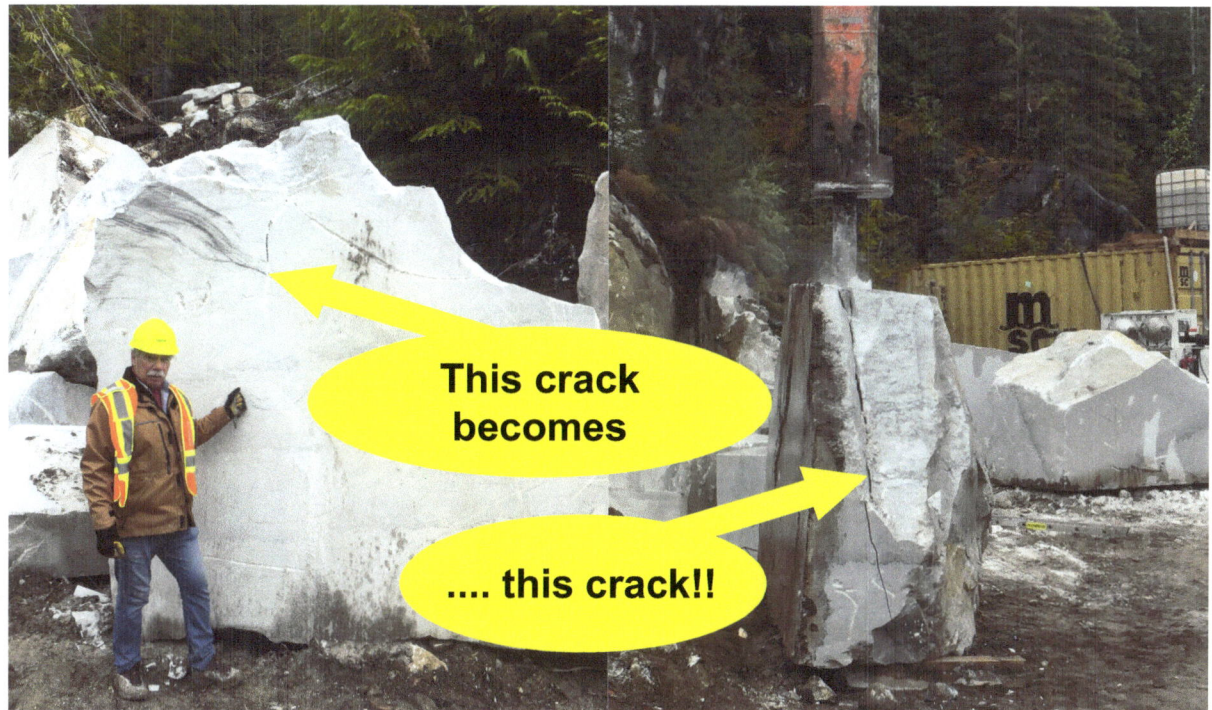

The original stone was a 44,000 pounder. That stone was a "second" Above left., you see a fault line going from top middle of the rock down almost through my head. As we prepared to move it down the mountain to the flatbed truck, I noticed that crack. My thought **"Just knock that piece off ..... it will just fall off later anyway ..... Right?"** We tried to knock off the small piece only to discover the real crack ...... on the right is a large jack hammer showing **"what the rock thought of my idea"**. In less than 5 seconds, the rock went from 44,000 lbs to 22,000 lbs. ...... 22,000 lbs crashed to the ground in a cloud of dust !!!

While the Volvo excavator's diesel engine screamed ....I internally screamed ...... as I walked away ..... some very angry expletives screamed under my breath ...... **"What the BLEEP am I going to do now?" ..... My design was useless!**

My choices? .... a) Choose another rock or b) go with the remaining 22,000 lbs. ...... But there was something in that original rock ..... I had chosen **THAT** rock ..... my name was on THAT rock ...... that rock was **MY ROCK!!**

Above right, you see the 10 tons that broke off. The flat face to the left is the remaining 22,000 lb rock. The hockey net, the parent and child would eventually be carved directly into that flat face. In the finished sculpture, the leading edge of the ice surface is the same flat face and the only remaining material from the 22,000 pound rock.

Big Rocks and the Stone Sculpture Myth

There is this myth that a sculptor, like Michelangelo, (or me …. willieangelo) "frees" a shape that lives within the rock …… bull!!!! …… imagine that two sculptors are thinking about what they will carve out of a 22 ton (44,000 lbs) rock. Even if the two artists were attempting to carve the exact same shape, little cracks (like my 10 ton crack), faults, missteps ….. all of those tiny things force the artist to move in one direction or another. In my case I went from a design with two grown men to a parent and child ….. A far simpler design!!!! …. Thank you Sir Marble! ……The stone is always the boss ….. the stone allows or denies the sculptor his or her design.

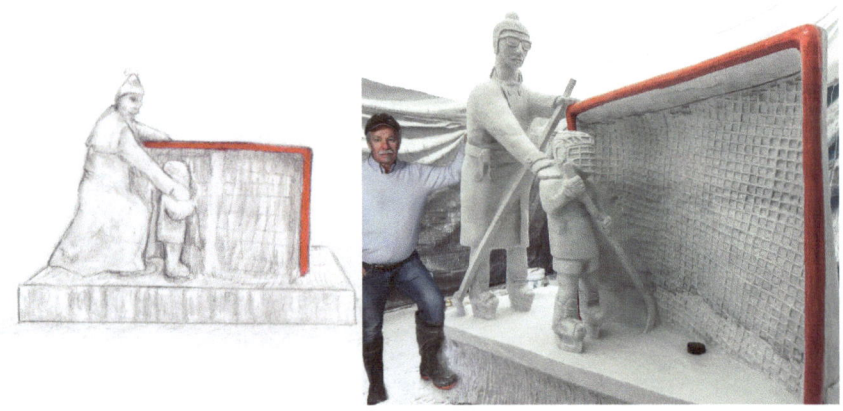

I attended a James Taylor concert during which he spoke of people asking him how he comes up with his songs. His response was "I really don't have any idea ….. I am just the first one to hear them".

People have asked me how I envisioned the design for "Creating a Champion"? …. Well …. It's sorta like James' answer …. the 10 tons fell to the ground ….. I did my little anger dance and …. within 1 minute of seeing my original design vanish in that cloud of dust ….. a new design popped into my head …… a design vision that ultimately turned into "Creating a Champion" ….. my rock **ALLOWED** me that vision ……

Without a word of a lie ….. I was "just the first to see it"!!!!

I had figured out the logistics ……. I had figured out how to get it to Red Deer …… but how to proceed was still a distant challenge …… things like "how do you carve the netting of a hockey net" or "how do you knit a toque in marble" or "how do you tie up kid's skates in marble" …… no idea ….. I often woke up in the middle of the night pondering questions of that sort!!!

What the heck was I thinking!!!

The Journey ... from British Columbia to Alberta

As I mentioned earlier, I struggled with how I was going to execute this dream that began back in 1974 but was now 100% in my face ..... REALITY!!!!

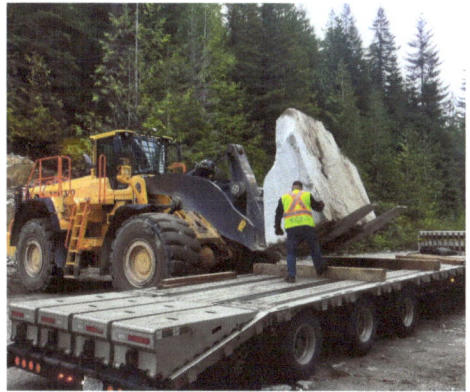

I found a trucking company, JT Hotshotting out of Delta B.C. In order to keep my costs down, JT would add my rock to another customer's shipment and it would be trucked out to Alberta when they had that other load. Soooo ..... Phase 1 done with! On the left is the Pacific West loader lifting my remaining 22,000 lbs onto the flatbed trailer.

I still needed to find a location to actually do the work! So ..... I created the poster (on the right) in order to convey to my colleagues at work the concept of this project. Darwin Sincennes at my work led me to Triple S Cranes who would lift the rock off the flatbed once it got to Red Deer. Triple S then led me to Trifecta Trucking who allowed me to work in their yard, carving outdoors from June through October ...... OK! ..... So now I have a location!!!! .... Pheww!

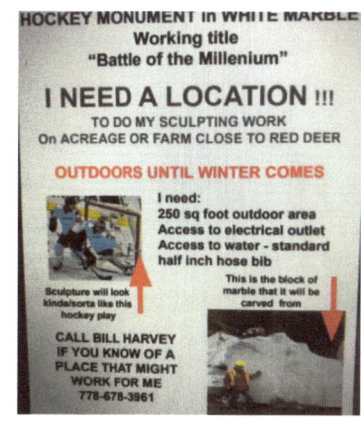

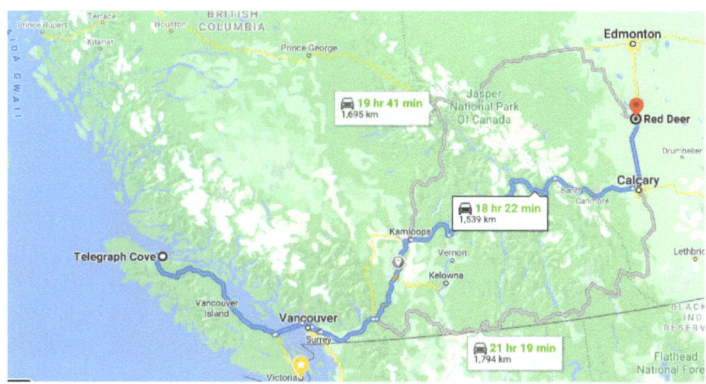

1,546 km from Vanouver Island to Red Deer where my rock was unloaded at the Trifecta yard.

Soooo ...... how does one even start??

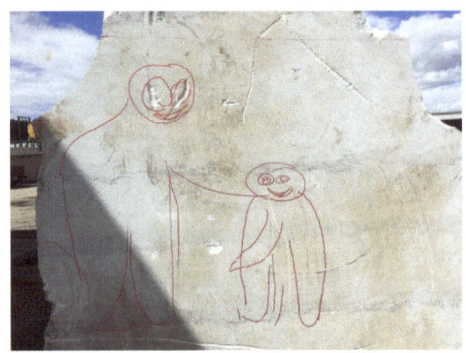

Recall, this is the "Just Do It" school of sculpture. So you see on the left, I just took a grease pencil and sketched out Champion "more or less" ... LOL!!

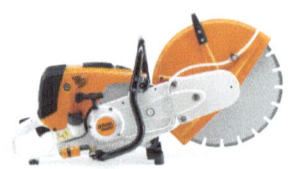

The Stihl concrete saw with a 12" blade, like the one above, did the lion's share of removing the bulk marble

Photo right, that's me approaching the stone's flat face with the Stihl concrete saw .... Double hearing protection, safety glasses, impact gloves, rubber boots ...... whether it is the heat in summer or the cold in winter ...... this is hot/cold, wet, noisy, physically demanding work ...... it's hard work!!

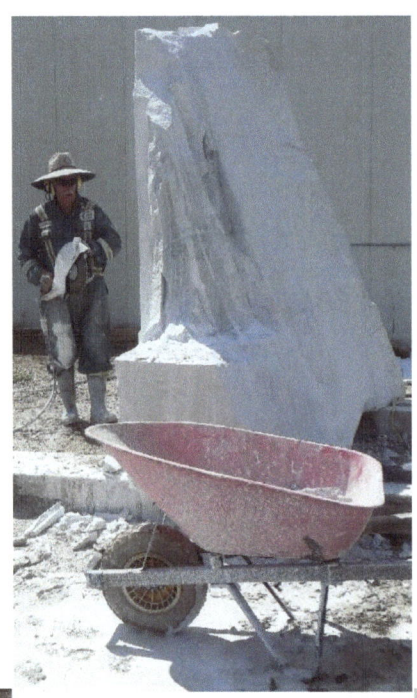

Photo below .... The first major cuts into the face of the rock. The square ultimately becomes the hockey net. The square post becomes the goal post. The flat face of the stone becomes the leading edge of the ice surface, the only original stone. The material above the square would be removed and becomes the top of the net.

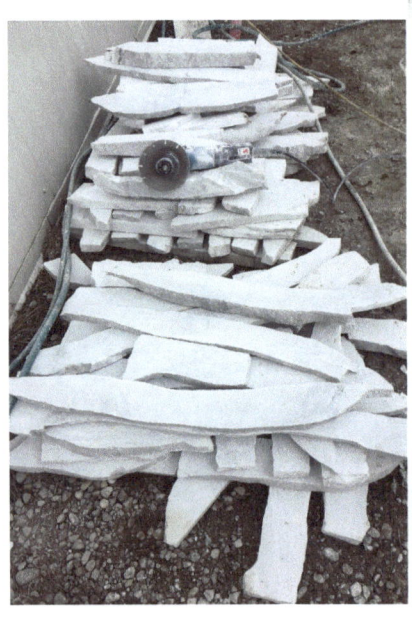

Photo left .... tons of marble slices that were carved off the 22,000 pound block. I gave the pieces away to people who used them in their yards and gardens in Red Deer ..... for walkways and things.

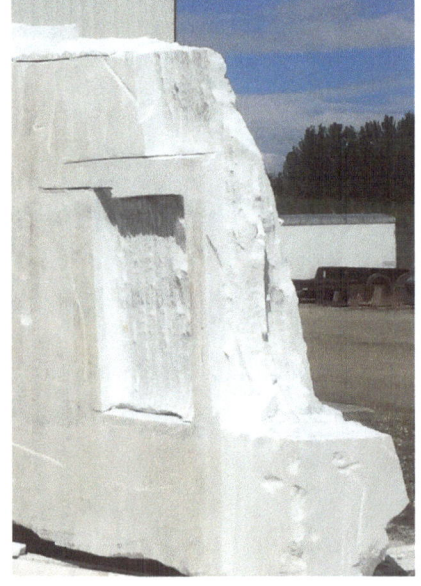

Brodie my model!!! …… thank you Brodie!!

Experienced sculptors envision 3-D shapes that they know they can do. As mentioned earlier, my experience was limited to some sand castles, a few wooden carvings in 2007-8 and a couple of test marble pieces in 2014-15. Relative to the "Creating a Champion" design, Angel and Lady of the the Lake were very simple to say the least.

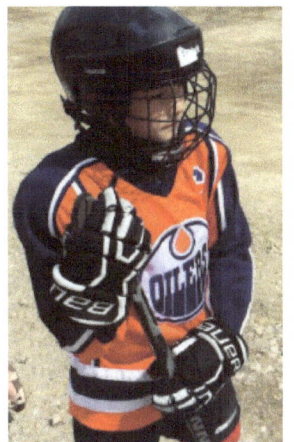
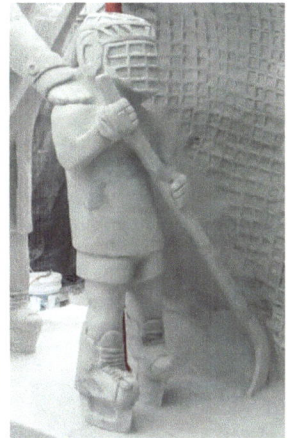
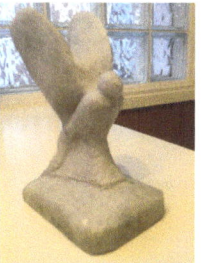
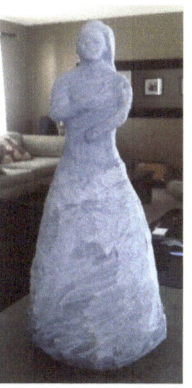

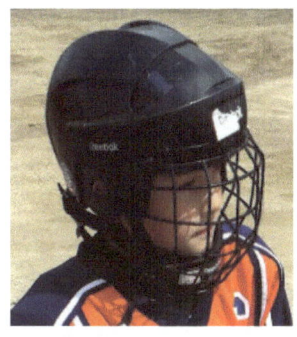

My first actions were to find life size models to help me in that visualizing. So as I started carving the big volumes of stone from the 22,000 pound rock, I started looking for a child model. My friend Josh had a friend Dean who had a 7 year old son Brodie …… an avid hockey player.

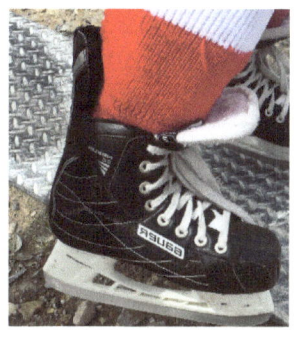

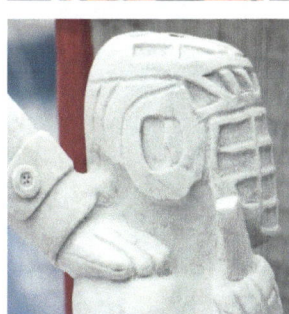

Brodie, Mom, Dad and Brodie's sister Summer all came over one day and we took these pictures. In between shots, Brodie and Summer couldn't help playing in the mud, picking up anything shiny that caught their fancy.

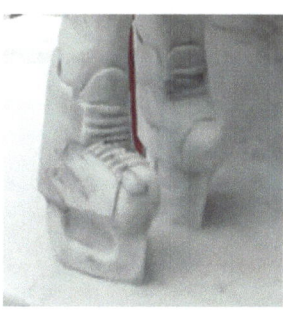

I am quite happy with the end result. Although not perfect by any means, the semblance delivers on my goal …. conveying the essence of supporting a child in their quest to be great …. the "Creating a Champion"!!

And so it goes …..
with ever smaller tools!!

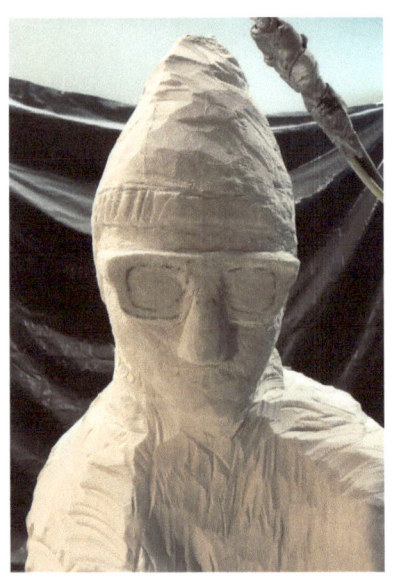
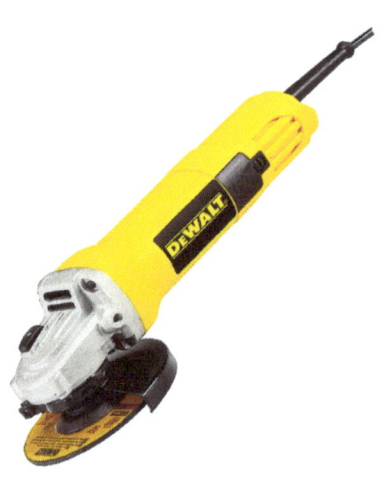
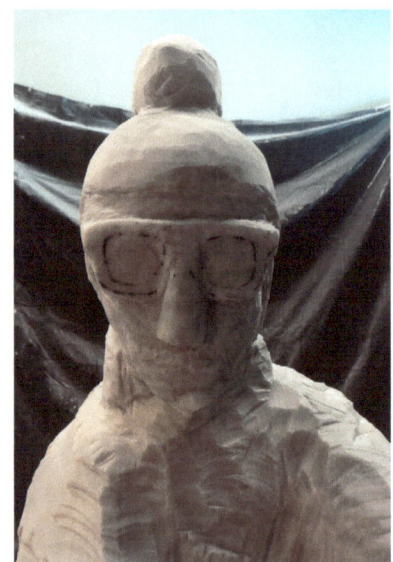

This form of sculpture is called "subtractive" because you take away material a little bit at a time. It was the middle of the "Year of COVID" and I lost track of how much time I was spending …… I was counting until I reached 1,200 hours.

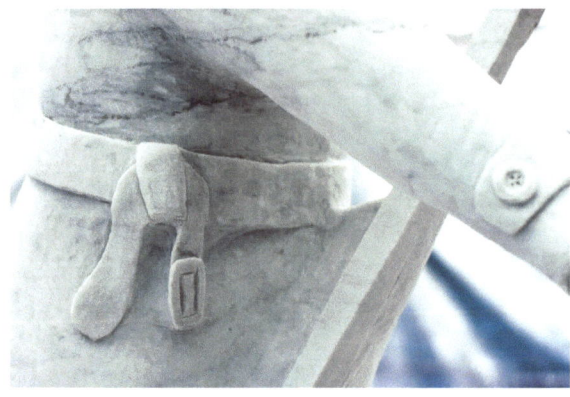

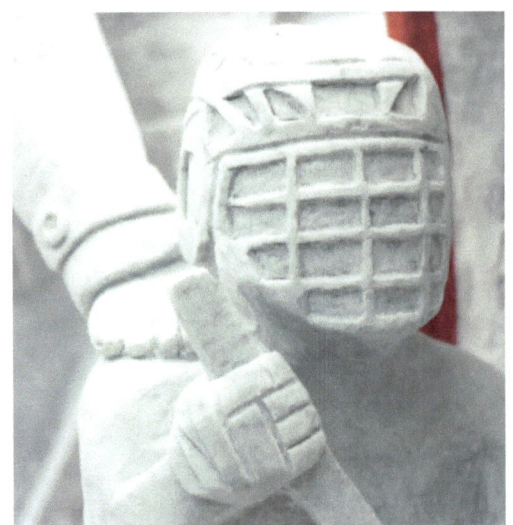

As the artist, in all of this work, I like the buttons and belt buckle the best !!!!

Here is how it goes ….. For real!!

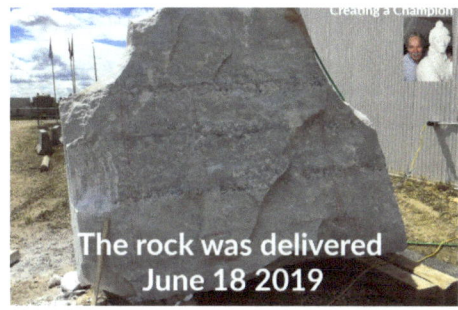

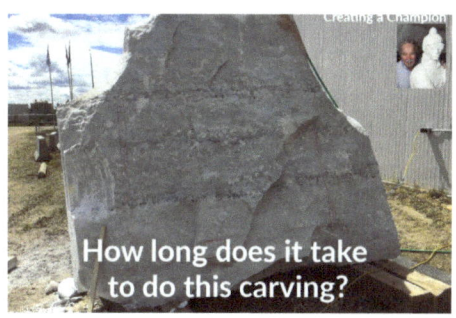

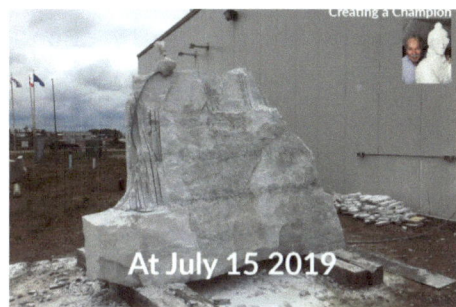

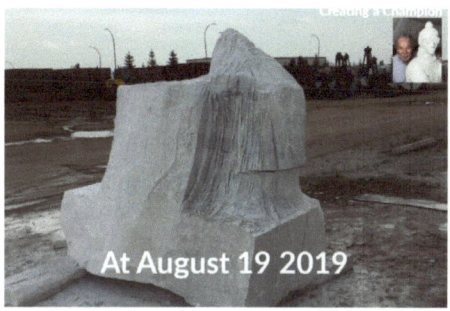

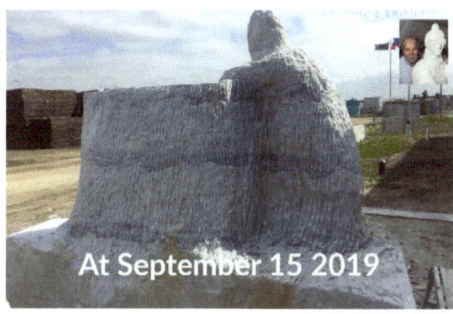

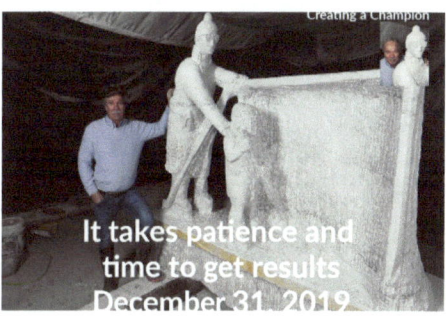

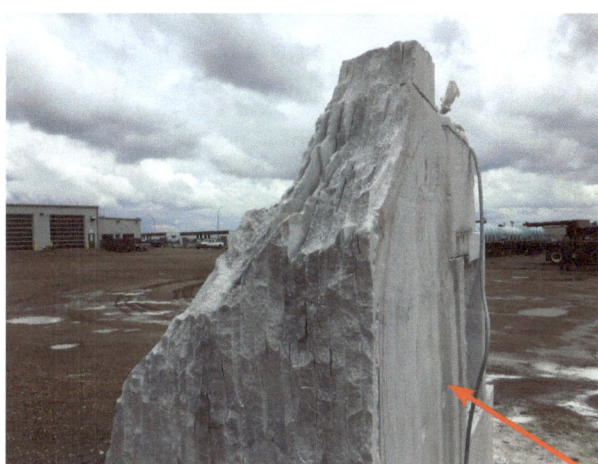

The leading edge of the ice surface is the only part of the rock's original flat surface that remains!!

Creating a Champion was completed in early June 2020 close to one year in the making. Each little square in the netting took 10-15 minutes!!!

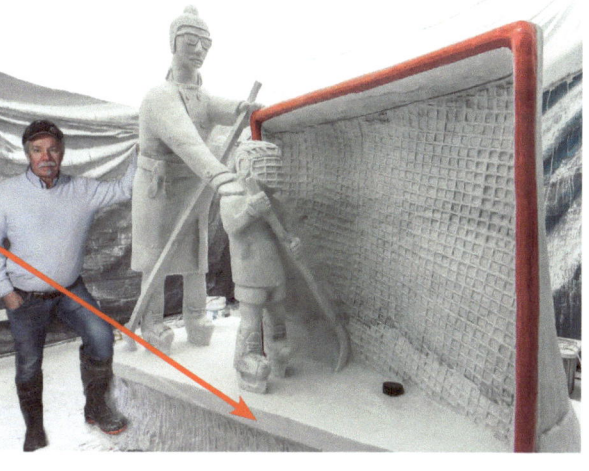

You can't really talk about 2020 and ignore COVID ….. I call it COVID DECAY!!

Covid Decay is the process by which COVID has and is still impacting the world. For me, maintaining the motivation to keep going was a huge hurdle!! ……… COVID DECAY!!

As a result of COVID and low oil prices, Calfrac decided that rather than lay off hundreds of people they would cut back on work hours which meant 2 weeks on and two weeks off for me. This allowed me more time to work on "Creating a Champion".

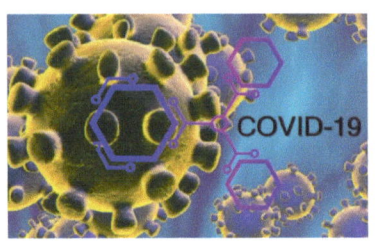

This period of time between January and March 2020 was one of the lowest emotional times in my life. On top of the hard, cold, wet work that is the reality of carving marble, COVID caused closures everywhere …… no restaurants ….. no bars ….. It felt like the world was a wasteland.

Finishing Champion was obviously a good thing ….. Actually doing it …. Maintaining the motivation …… A whole other thing!

You have lots of time to think while doing this work. Thoughts around COVID were not positive thoughts. I would think about what happens next for me, for the company, for Canada, for the world? …. COVID DECAY!! ….. What job would I do? ….. COVID DECAY!! …… Where would I go for lunch? ….. COVID DECAY!! …… Where might I go (everything was closed) ….. COVID DECAY!! …… I reached very depressed states of mind for many, many days ……. COVID DECAY!!

It was a very difficult time! The thought of abandoning Champion was often present!! If it wasn't for the reality of "what the heck would the landlord do with a 4.5 ton rock?" …. LOL!!! …. The thought that Champion might forever be relegated to a garbage heap somewhere in Red Deer was the main driver that got me out of that funk. My original goal was that Champion be displayed somewhere that it would be appreciated ….. maybe even inspirational ……the question ….. if I didn't find "that place" for Champion, who would?

So despite Covid, the hard work, the cold, the wet, the noise ….. I was able to keep going and bring the project to completion in early June 2020 ….. Almost exactly one year from the day that my rock arrived in Red Deer!!!! It was a proud moment for me to look upon the finished piece …… a huge accomplishment ……

"I did it!!"

My estimate of Champion's final weight was 9 - 10,000 pounds. After all was said and done …… it started at 44,000 lbs …… then down to 22,000 lbs at the quarry (see page 11) ….. to the final tally ….. 9,351 lbs …… pretty good guess I would say ….. LOL

The Final Chapters

So I did it ….. now what? ….. what does one do with a 4.5 ton sculpture that nobody has expressed any interest in ….. whatever the shape it is carved into ….. I was paying rent on a building, albeit minimal rent, and was unemployed …… Covid was still the major issue on people's minds …… I was unable to find anyone to take an interest in the piece. So I decided that I would wrap it up and store it in the same Trifecta yard where I had started the carving a year earlier. I got permission to do that ….. I did a trip to the Maritimes in Canada with some friends ….. followed that with a trip to San Carlos, Mexico ….. somewhere down in Mexico I actually contracted Covid ….. returned to Canada …… Champion was the last thing on my mind for more than 6 months!!

Until one morning …. January 2021 …. rolling around in bed …. a sleepless night …. a thought ….. "Just give Champion away" ….. "Just give it away for free" …. rather than leave it all wrapped up …. under a tarp …. in the Trifecta yard ….. **so how might that work?**

I put an advertisement in the FREE section of Kijiji.ca the free classified web site …… "FREE Marble Hockey monument" … and OMG, I was inundated with responses from men and women all over Alberta.!

The responses were primarily sincere interest but a few were pretty special ….. one guy wondered if he could install it in the window of his barber shop ….. another had a hockey fan neighbour ….. he thought it would be a great joke to just drop it on his neighbour's lawn ….. I can't imagine the humour once the reality set it.

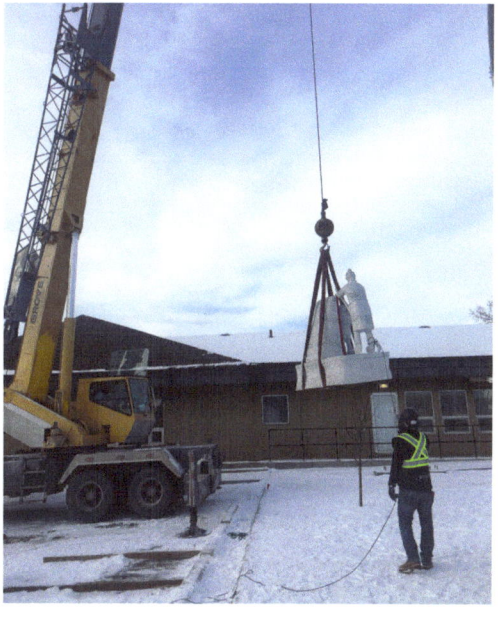

Another wondered if he could just "stop by and pick it up ….. well ….. here is what it takes to "just pick it up"!!!! On the right is the crane bringing Champion to its new home at the Parkland Community Association rink in Calgary.

Just like when I first committed to my 44,000 pound rock ….. most people just cannot fathom what it takes to work with such a huge weight ….. You learn very quickly that you better have thought through your plan …. It is all very real!!

Creating a Champion is finally at home!!

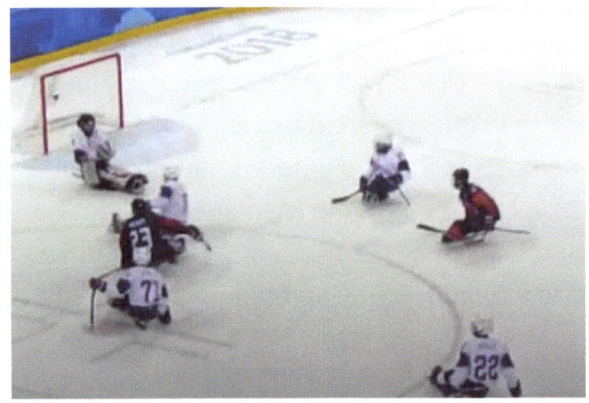

Turns out that on the morning of January 3, 2021, Global News had run a segment about the Parkdale Community Association in Calgary and their sledge hockey rink. The rink is designed and built as the first outdoor sledge hockey rink in Western Canada.

One of the first people who had seen my ad and responded suggested that I should look them up and ….. I did! …… and that is how Champion found its new home at the Parkdale Community rink in Calgary Alberta.

Mr. Andy Thiessen was the Director of Operations at the Parkdale Community Association. We talked and arranged for him to come see Champion. After a whole lot of negotiating between myself, Andy, the City of Calgary and the Board of the Parkdale Association, an agreement was reached and voila ….. Champion's new home!!!

Champion is being donated to Parkdale by the Thiessen family - Andy, Kristin, Kaiden, Beckett and Lily.

I am a big Beatles fan …. one of my favorite songs is "The Long and Winding Road" (https://www.youtube.com/watch?v=fR4HjTH_fTM). My marble rock has taken a long and winding road to find its new home ……. from my imagination's journey seeing Michelangelo's Pieta in 1974 ….. to the marble quarry in British Columbia ….. to Red Deer Alberta ….. to more than 1,200 hours of blood, swear and tears …. to Kijiji ….. to the Thiessen family ….. to the Parkland Community Association's sledge hockey rink in Calgary!

About the Sculptor!

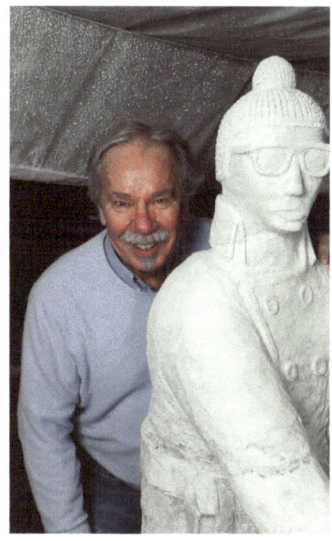

Bill was born in Sherbrooke Quebec and grew up in North Bay Ontario. In 1977, after completing a Bachelor's degree in Economics from the University of Guelph, he moved to Edmonton Alberta.

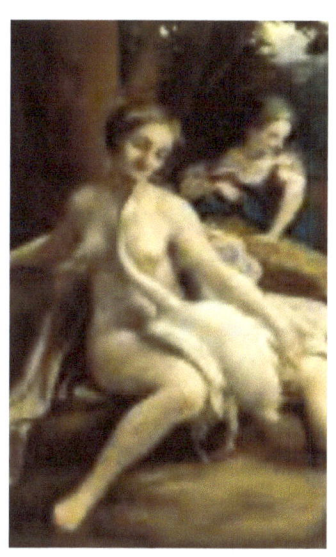

Since then he has followed different opportunities providing him with experience in Oil and Gas, Transportation, Healthcare, Clinical research, Sales and Marketing including online training and development ….. and of course sculpture ….. he is presently planning his next sculpture ….. a mythological story, bas-relief based on Corregio's "Leda and he Swan" (above right) ….

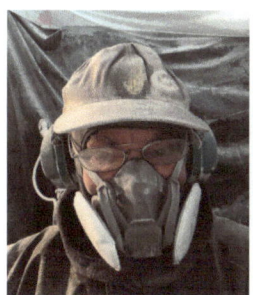 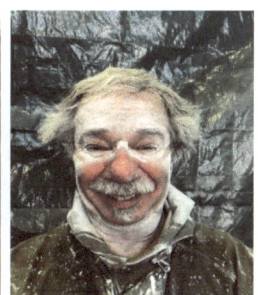

To the right, Bill enjoys being a bit of clown ...With and without mask, after a hard day's work!

Bill is divorced and has two adult children who live in British Columbia.

He lived in Red Deer Alberta from 2017 to 2020 while carving "Creating a Champion". Then in Quebec CIty, for six months in 2021 and is now back in British Columbia Canada.

You can reach him at bharveyvictoria@gmail.com

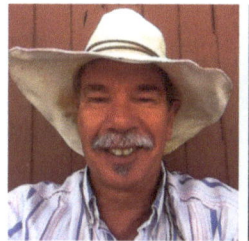 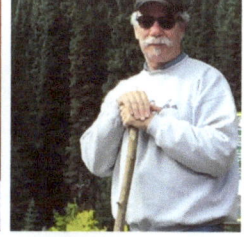
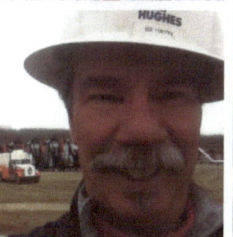 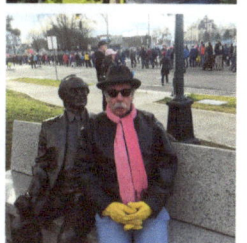

Thank You!!

I would like to thank all of those who provided all kinds of support to me in completing "Creating A Champion" and making this project a success! Without you I would never have been able to maintain the physical and emotional strengths needed to bring Champion to fruition ….

    Wayne and Heather Harvey   Susan Willmott
    Mona Harvey   Teresa White
    Phil Koch   Brody Dawson
    Granquartz- all the guys there   Dean Dawson and family
    Dale Harvey   Connie and Guy
    Patricia Chapman   Marvin Sandstra
    Belle Tuckerman   Mike Russo Photography
    Toyota Yaris   Tim Seibel
    Patricia Tuckey   Steve Blanke - Triple S Crane
    Gene Wiebe - Trifecta Transport   Aaron Alstrom
    Kevin Landry   Guy Garret
    Ken Jensen   John Neil
    Josh Young   Gary Rettenheimer
    JT Hotshotting   Dave Sparky
    Linda Leonard   Danielle Klooster
    Grace Hovious Photography   Darwin Sinsennes
    Carol Sylvan   Seun Edunjobi - Book Designer
    Albert Lebeau   Maurice Harvey

To all those that I have not noted here ….. my sincerest apology!
I thank you too and apologize for missing your name here!!!

(It is a pain getting old and forgetful - LOL!!!)

www.ingramcontent.com/pod-product-compliance
Lightning Source LLC
Chambersburg PA
CBHW051840210526
45473CB00005B/1953